Coffee Table Quick Tips:

Weekly Training Tips for Firehouse Coffee Table Discussions

Commitment, Camaraderie, Caffeine

Author – AB Turenne

Foreword by Chief James P. Trzaski

ISBN 979-8-89309-432-9 (Paperback)
ISBN 979-8-89309-433-6 (Digital)

Copyright © 2024 Author – AB Turenne
All rights reserved
First Edition

All rights reserved. No part of this publication may be reproduced, distributed, or transmitted in any form or by any means, including photocopying, recording, or other electronic or mechanical methods without the prior written permission of the publisher. For permission requests, solicit the publisher via the address below.

Covenant Books
11661 Hwy 707
Murrells Inlet, SC 29576
www.covenantbooks.com

FOREWORD

I have been involved in the fire service for a cumulative forty years since first volunteering in 1985. Throughout my career, I have had many opportunities to meet a wide array of people. My experiences include being a volunteer and career firefighter, a company officer, and the chief of a department.

During my tenure, like many of my peers and mentors, I became a fire service instructor. This role afforded a wide array of opportunities for me as an instructor, and it soon became clear that this was the avenue for me to demonstrate and satisfy my passion for the fire service. The exposure that I received as an instructor led me to become the director of a regional fire school and an instructor for the Connecticut Fire Academy as a lead recruit instructor. Currently, I am the chief of department for the South Fire District, City of Middletown, Connecticut.

The South Fire District is where I first met AB when he came to our department as an entry-level firefighter. It was apparent that he had a drive and passion for the fire service. AB was not new to the fire service; however, he was new to our organization. Those of you who are fire service members can appreciate the culture of our trade. Becoming a probie matters not of your past experiences and credentials; you are being sized up daily by how you perform for us.

Many members appreciated AB's drive and passion, and as you can imagine, some did not. He quickly engaged in every part of our department and embraced "the brotherhood." He continuously invests time and energy to promote our department and is involved in all union and department functions. Over time, he was able to utilize his passion and drive to influence others. Never sitting on the bench, AB is constantly seeking new ways to engage others while promoting training, safety, and a love for the job.

He has had an instrumental impact in a short period of time and now serves in the role of Captain of Training and Safety. Many of the programs he has implemented have created opportunities for the fire service to unite and collaborate. His unwavering commitment to spreading the message, promoting "the job," and staying true to his convictions is inspiring.

AB's engagement in conversation and creating relationships has enhanced the culture of our department. *Coffee Table Quick Tips* is that book that will start engagements and conversations at the fire department coffee table through his collection of small tips and tricks being shared throughout the fire service community.

This compilation brings subject material to a single-page discussion point. The reader can now explore the subject more in depth and create a company drill or discussion. I am honored to write this foreword for Captain Turenne, and I fully endorse and appreciate his drive to share what has been shared with him during his tenure. I strongly encourage readers to use this publication as a foundation for some "Coffee Table Quick Tips" for their own organizations.

In the interest of the fire service and brotherhood.

—Chief James P. Trzaski

PREFACE

Some of the best learning experiences on the job come from the confines and comfort of the back of the apparatus bay or at the kitchen table at the firehouse over a cup of coffee.

It's these interactions that allow the senior man on shift to display his institutional knowledge and wisdom on the new guys while in turn providing an atmosphere and opportunity for all on shift, regardless of rank or tenure, to start the dialogue that leads to the passing of information that becomes quick tips of information.

This compilation of *Coffee Table Quick Tips* is a collection of fire service facets of informal education that were articulated to me by those who have had a direct impact and influence on the growth and development of my fire service journey over the past twenty-five years as a firefighter in Eastern Connecticut.

Over those years, many tips of the trade that were passed along to me have come from a wide array of company officers and firefighters from a mixture of volunteer, industrial, and career departments.

Often, these snapshots of wisdom have been implemented and have played a significant role in what has become a successful career, leading me to where I am today.

Throughout the following pages, you will come across a total of fifty-two Coffee Table Quick Tips, which in turn provide a single tip for each week of the year that can easily be implemented into a training curriculum within your department or can be used solely for the purpose of sharing among those who make up the complement of your current group or platoon.

Increasing the overall human capital knowledge of yourself will lead the way for you to become an asset on the fireground. Sharing this same knowledge with your peers will aid in increasing the capital knowledge of all.

If one Coffee Table Quick Tip from this collection helps you along the way, then all of the work put forth with creating this book was worth the time. It is our responsibility as part of the brotherhood to continue passing down what we have learned from those who came before us.

Contents

Coffee Table Quick Tips (January 1 to June 30)

Week 1: Motor Vehicle Accident Size-Up Considerations 1
Week 2: Wheel Chocks at Motor Vehicle Accidents 3
Week 3: Extrication Elements for School Transportation.............5
Week 4: Patient Compartment Access, Taking the Window.........6
Week 5: Pinned Foot, *No* Tool 8
Week 6: The Halligan Hook, from the Roof to RIT Part 1 9
Week 7: The Halligan Hook, from the Roof to RIT Part 2 11
Week 8: The Halligan Hook, from the Roof to RIT Part 3 12
Week 9: Fountain Soda and the Fire Service...............................14
Week 10: Recycle, Repurpose, Reuse Part 1 16
Week 11: Recycle, Repurpose, Reuse Part 2 18
Week 12: Recycle, Repurpose, Reuse Part 3 19
Week 13: Logical Ladder Lengths 20
Week 14: Pocket of Pliers Part 1..22
Week 15: Pocket of Pliers Part 2..23
Week 16: Pocket of Pliers Part 3..24
Week 17: The Spring Clamp Part 1 25
Week 18: The Spring Clamp Part 2 27
Week 19: The Spring Clamp Part 3 29
Week 20: Ground Ladder Basics Part 1 30
Week 21: Ground Ladder Basics Part 2 31
Week 22: Ground Ladder Basics Part 3 32
Week 23: The Tachometer Acronym 33
Week 24: Estimating the Stretch Part 1 35
Week 25: Estimating the Stretch Part 2 37
Week 26: Estimating the Stretch Part 3 38

Coffee Table Quick Tips
(July 1 to December 31)

Week 27: Size Up Variables from the Driveway Part 1 39
Week 28: Size Up Variables from the Driveway Part 2 40
Week 29: Size Up Variables from the Driveway Part 3 41
Week 30: Size Up Variables from the Driveway Part 42
Week 31: Building Construction, Creating Search Aides Part 1 ...44
Week 32: Building Construction, Creating Search Aides Part 2 ...45
Week 33: Practice Like You Play Part 1 47
Week 34: Practice Like You Play Part 2 49
Week 35: Practice Like You Play Part 3 51
Week 36: Practice Like You Play Part 4 52
Week 37: Bleach Bottle of Rope..53
Week 38: Stair Stretches..55
Week 39: Water Supply, at Nine O'clock 56
Week 40: Tool Trick Part 1 58
Week 41: Tool Trick Part 2 60
Week 42: Tool Trick Part 3 61
Week 43: Tool Trick Part 4 62
Week 44: Gemtor Harness and SCBA Conversion.......................64
Week 45: Pre-Rigged Hauling System for a Downed Firefighter ..66
Week 46: Identifying Bedroom Windows During Size Up 68
Week 47: Commercial Roof Structure—Creating Saw Access 70
Week 48: Identifying a Parapet from Below 72
Week 49: Existing Drainage, Water Removal from the Structure..73
Week 50: The Thermal Imaging Camera for Open Water Spills...75
Week 51: Brown Smoke, Bad Building 76
Week 52: The "Odor Unfounded" Call for Service 78

WEEK 1

Motor Vehicle Accident Size-Up Considerations

The initial size up of any incident sets the tone for the duration of the call, which is why it is so imperative to determine precisely what you are about to be presented with.

Your crew is likely to dismount the apparatus with a different mindset and demeanor after hearing a "two car rear with all occupants out of the vehicles" than they would with a reported head-on with extensive front-end intrusion and possible fire in the engine compartment.

Your preliminary report to dispatch, arriving units, and your crew will trigger their sense of urgency about what hazards to be mindful of as well as what tools and equipment are going to be needed.

For you, as the company officer or senior firefighter, the initial size up should include and determine the following:

- number of vehicles involved
- type of accident or mechanism (rear-end impact, head-on, roll-over, etc.)
- number of occupants (walking wound vs. entrapment)
- potential fire or explosion
- presence of hazardous materials (contents stored and/or involved)
- size and weight of vehicle (commercial cab, sedan, motorcycle)
- potential for mass occupancy (school buses, coach buses, etc.)
- utilities involved (overhead powerlines or underground services)
- structures involved (house, commercial property, and pole/sign)
- vehicle submerged in water, ejected occupant in the water, or extrication near water
- need for additional resources (heavy wrecker, additional ambulance, or second tool)

WEEK 2

Wheel Chocks at Motor Vehicle Accidents

With the rise of both hybrid and electric vehicles, it is imperative that firefighters implement chocking wheels even for motor vehicles that are stable on all four tires.

The likelihood that a hybrid or electric vehicle could still move in a horizontal fashion is high due to the vehicle's components and our inability to ensure that *all* power is secured and the system will not activate while we are investigating the incident or tending to the patient(s).

The following are best practices to ensure the safety of those on scene:

Avoid approaching the potential path of travel by approaching the motor vehicle from the side and chocking a wheel *prior* to performing other tasks.

Wooden wheel chocks with a minimum of 4" in height are the most optimal. Do *not* use wedges or two-by-four-inch chocks because they do *not* create enough resistance for motor vehicle tires.

If all four wheels are contacting the ground, pick *any* wheel to chock (it doesn't matter which wheel is chocked); however, the safest practice is to chock more than one wheel based on the position and elevation of the motor vehicle.

You can *never* assume that the vehicle won't move!

WEEK 3

Extrication Elements for School Transportation

The three black lines running along the side of school buses are more than merely decorative in nature; in fact, they are part of the structural integrity of the school bus and are referred to as *rub rails*, which are in place to meet crash test and safety requirements.

While the exact positioning of the rub rails might vary from manufacturer to manufacturer, they can be used as a great reference point for extrication purposes when warranted during a motor vehicle accident involving a school bus.

Black line location identification:

1. top of the seats
2. bottom of the seats
3. level of the floor

WEEK 4

Patient Compartment Access, Taking the Window

Oftentimes, you will find yourself needing to take (or break) a window of a motor vehicle when the door is locked or damaged in an effort to gain access to the passenger compartment, whether it is for occupant removal or for other means of investigation.

While some firefighters carry window punches on their person, I have witnessed over the years that people either misplace them or forget they have the punch and revert to using a hand tool such as a Halligan bar to take the glass.

This week's Coffee Table Quick Tip illustrates an easy yet effective way to take the glass in a controlled manner by utilizing the adze end of a Halligan bar.

Using the following means prevents a firefighter from using the baseball bat swing, which could potentially come into contact with a patient trapped on the opposite side, and it also leads to loose glass becoming a projectile.

1. Ensure that the door is either locked or inoperable.
2. Force the adze end of the Halligan bar down into the door behind the rubber gasket at the base of the window.
3. Using the leverage of the bar, gently push down toward the door/ground, and the window will shatter.
4. Using a gloved hand, lightly push away the shattered glass, with patient safety remaining paramount at all times.

WEEK 5

Pinned Foot, *No* Tool

Often, we will find ourselves responding to motor vehicle accidents that require the use of extrication equipment for gaining entry to a passenger compartment, such as the driver's seat, due to impact and damage.

Implementing the use of hydraulic spreaders contributes to a positive outcome when you have adequate room for positioning and placement from the exterior of a vehicle.

What happens once the door is popped and the operator's foot is pinned beneath or behind the brake pedal and you don't have available space for placement of the spreaders or the tools at hand malfunction?

That's when we rely on what is in our pockets and revert back to the basics of extrication fundamentals that were used prior to the invention of cutters such as the Holmatro CU 4007 C mini cutters.

By simply wrapping the steel arm of the brake pedal (as low as you can to the pedal) with a girth hitch in a shot of 1" tubular webbing, you (or with assistance if needed) can pull the opposing end up or outward, in turn bending the steel arm and creating the needed gap to remove the foot of the trapped operator.

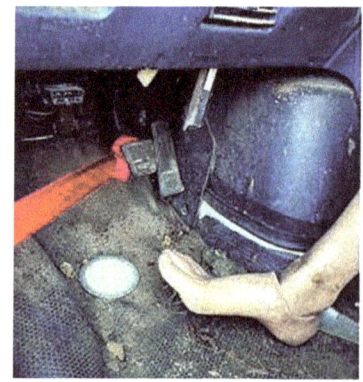

WEEK 6

The Halligan Hook, from the Roof to RIT Part 1

With typical household construction, windowsills are found to be three feet from the floor. When attempting to raise and lift a downed firefighter up and over a windowsill to a ladder, their combined body weight and gear, along with a cumbersome position, can prove to be extremely difficult to do under duress.

With a Halligan hook, a shot of 11-mm cord, and two carabiners, a mechanical advantage can be created and applied to assist with lifting the downed firefighter up and over the sill and into the hands of a firefighter waiting on the top rungs of a thrown ladder.

To accomplish this, wrap the terminal end of the 11-mm cord around the shaft where the two angled ends meet. Two to three wraps should be sufficient to secure the cord in place via friction once weight is added to the cord.

On the end of the terminal end (figure 8 on a bite), attach a carabiner. Next, feed the portion of the working end through the carabiner and capture it with an oversized carabiner.

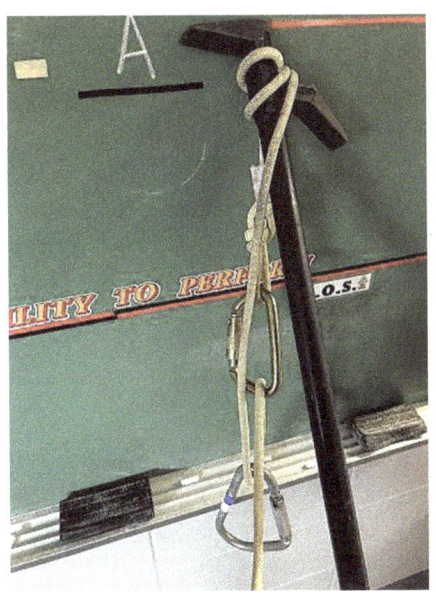

In the ensemble pictured to the left, the oversized carabiner is used, as the mechanical advantage is from an out-of-service Gemtor harness. The larger size allows you to manipulate the carabiner easier with the limited dexterity of a gloved hand and can be fed through the rear of an SCBA much quicker.

With the 6' Halligan hook resting on an angle against the window frame, one firefighter can pull the 11-mm cord down and assist with lifting the downed firefighter off the floor while another firefighter guides him/her to the top of the sill and out to awaiting firefighters.

WEEK 7

The Halligan Hook, from the Roof to RIT Part 2

Utilizing two Halligan hooks and the existing frame/straps of the downed firefighter's Self-Contained Breathing Apparatus (SCBA), an effective and efficient means of converting the hooks into a portable litter will allow for two firefighters to lift and carry the downed firefighter up and over obstacles and/or void spaces in the floor and can be used as a rapid means of egressing up or down a set of stairs.

After confirming the downed firefighter's air supply and silencing their Personal Alert Safety System (PASS) device, feed the pry end of the hook through the shoulder strap and waist strap, starting at the left side of the firefighter's head.

Continue next by doing the same from the firefighter's right side of the head, cinching down on all the straps, and adding a simple overhand knot.

The last step is to lift and place the lower extremities (legs) up and over the hook, as shown in the photograph above.

By bending and utilizing your legs, you and your partner can grab the ends of the hooks and lift the downed firefighter as you would with a backboard or pole stretcher.

WEEK 8

The Halligan Hook, from the Roof to RIT Part 3

When met with conditions that warrant you to push or drag a downed firefighter along an open floor space or a long hallway, a mechanical advantage combined with the Halligan hook can add ease to the operation as well as shave off time by removing the downed firefighter out of an Immediately Dangerous to Life or Health (IDLH) environment and into the hands of Emergency Medical Services (EMS) personnel.

With two firefighters at the downed firefighter, providing adequate air supply and performing a rapid assessment on the extent of potential injuries, a single pulley can be fixed to the top of the SCBA shoulder straps via a short shot of 1" tubular webbing and an oversized carabiner. This task can be performed with limited visibility due to smoke conditions and with the limited dexterity of a gloved hand by having the equipment staged as shown in the photo below.

At the doorway and egress point of the structure, another firefighter can be staged with the terminal end (figure 8 on a bite) connected to a Halligan hook that is resting across the threshold in a secured fashion.

This simple mechanical advantage allows a downed firefighter to be hauled horizontally with limited manpower and limited equipment.

As the firefighter at the anchor point (Halligan hook) hauls the line, the two with the downed firefighter can push and drive in sync by placing the legs of the downed firefighter over each of their shoulders. At the same time, they are able to monitor the downed firefighter's condition and move any obstacles, such as furniture or debris, out of the path of travel.

WEEK 9

Fountain Soda and the Fire Service

Establishments within your response area that serve fountain soda as a beverage option (fast food restaurants, breweries, and diners) utilize carbon dioxide (CO_2) for the carbonation process, which mixes CO_2 and flavored syrup that results in some of our favorites, such as Sprite and cola.

CO_2, like propane, is heavier than air and will accumulate easily in areas such as basements, storage rooms, and compartments within the confines of a restaurant. Most often, CO_2 leaks occur from damaged plastic piping that is used to transport the gas and/or the mixed product to the soda fountain machine.

Symptoms of exposure to CO_2 can appear as follows:

- Headaches
- Difficulty breathing
- Increased heart rate
- Dizziness
- Sweating
- Convulsions
- Restlessness
- Malaise

For this week's *Coffee Table Quick Tip*, remember when responding to an EMS call to a place that serves fountain soda and/or beer from a tap that a best practice is to implement the use of a 4-gas meter when the signs and symptoms listed above present themselves.

While a 4-gas meter does *not* monitor the presence of CO_2 in the atmosphere, it will, however, make you aware of an oxygen-depletion atmosphere.

These incidents should be considered a hazardous materials response, with firefighters donning *all* of their personal protective equipment (PPE), including a self-contained breathing apparatus (SCBA).

Week 10

Recycle, Repurpose, Reuse Part 1

As Gemtor harnesses are subjected to wear and tear, eventually causing them to be taken out of service, the large carabiners still have a use, specifically in assisting with the rapid removal of a downed firefighter.

Once taken out of service, cut the oversized carabiner free from the harness and remove the lanyard pin from the device. Keep a cache of these leftover capturing devices on hand, and you can put them into action in high-stress and limited-visibility situations, even with the restricted dexterity of your gloved hand. The following use is a great Coffee Table Quick Tip that can easily be implemented for the use of lifting a downed firefighter up and over a set of risers while ascending stairs.

Many firefighters have been taught a method of carrying a downed firefighter up a flight of stairs and to safety (more than likely from a basement or below grade) by using two firefighters. But trying to grab under the SCBA straps themselves can inadvertently cause the downed firefighter to free themselves from the SCBA harness, causing this lift and move to be more difficult to perform. By syncing down the shoulder straps of the SCBA and capturing the harness at the back of the neck, where both shoulder straps meet, the oversized carabiner will act as a handle that is easier to grab and lift.

    Firefighters must be able to adapt and overcome. Being resourceful with our equipment can prove to be a great way of extending its life and, if needed, helping to extend the life of one of our own.

WEEK 11

Recycle, Repurpose, Reuse Part 2

A disadvantage to the shape and size of the RIT-Pak is that they can become quite cumbersome during the removal of the downed firefighter.

By locating two capture points on the RIT-Pak (Scott RIT-Pak III has solid rings attached on both sides of the housing unit, for example) and connecting the oversized carabiners in advance, the pre-staged carabiners can now be easily manipulated by a gloved hand to secure the Pak to the torso of the downed firefighter.

Simply capture the shoulder straps of their SCBA harness on each side. This will now secure the RIT-Pak in place and free up a firefighter to help clear debris or move the downed firefighter to safety.

WEEK 12

Recycle, Repurpose, Reuse Part 3

Part of the tool cache that many RIT groups assemble consists of a basket (stokes) or backboard to help in the removal of a downed or injured firefighter. I like to use a folding/attic ladder equipped with two oversized carabiners connected three rungs down from the top. By placing the downed firefighter face down with their regulator and face piece through the rungs, you can secure them to the ladder by connecting their shoulder straps to the ladder with the carabiners.

The ladder acts as a solid carrying surface and makes for an easy lift when moving up and over debris or down long corridors and hallways without jeopardizing their SCBA mask regulator.

WEEK 13

Logical Ladder Lengths

Ladders play an essential role on the fireground, even when you are *not* assigned as the truck company conducting ventilation efforts or performing rescue measures.

Often, those operating as the engine company find themselves having to work a hoseline up a ladder and into a window or void space. When allocated as the Rapid Intervention Team (RIT), a critical initial on-scene step (following a size up and 360) is to "soften the building" by laddering all of the windows and egress points.

Regardless of the apparatus you respond with or the task you are assigned to, being intimately familiar with ladders and their limitations can make their deployment more effective and efficient.

A great Coffee Table Quick Tip that can easily be implemented on the fireground for choosing which ladder to grab and throw is as follows: When selecting a ladder, grab a ladder with the first number of the length that matches the floor in which you need to reach or, in some instances, the roof immediately above the floor.

- 14' ladder: first floor or roof line above (example: single story ranch)
- 24' ladder: second floor (example: colonial style home)
- 35' ladder: third floor (example: triple decker multi-family)

When conducting a rescue from a window, the ladder *only* needs to reach the sill.

WEEK 14

Pocket of Pliers Part 1

Locking pliers are a cost-effective means of using a common tool from the labor trade and can easily be improvised for purposes within the fire service. These pliers (which are commonly referred to by the brand name Vise Grip) can be purchased at any local hardware store and are stocked at all major big box stores such as Home Depot and Lowes, with prices averaging from $20 to $300 depending on how much you are willing to spend.

With two simple variations (replacing the set bolt with an eyebolt and attaching a lanyard), the locking pliers can discreetly be carried within a pocket on your turnout gear.

No matter if the garage or overhead door is opened via manual means or with the use of an electric door opener, the possibility of the door closing after firefighters gain access for search or suppression efforts is high. The option of staging a lone firefighter at the door is counterintuitive to fireground operations when that able body could be put to use to meet the objective.

By simply locking the pliers to the door rail directly below where the bottom of the door rests in the open position, the door will *not* close on a charged hoseline or trap the firefighters in the garage or warehouse space should the door springs fail.

WEEK 15

Pocket of Pliers Part 2

Oftentimes, when performing standpipe operations, we are faced with systems that are missing the handwheel needed to open or shut the standpipe's gate valve. The valves are *not* maintained properly and are damaged by outside exposure (parking garage systems) or purposely damaged by the hands of vandals.

When confronted with this dilemma, quick access to a pair of locking pliers can act as a makeshift handle to operate the valve when water is needed in a timely manner. This can easily be accomplished by clamping the locking pliers to the exposed valve stem and turning it in a counterclockwise motion to open when water is called for. The same method can also be applied should the handle or handwheel on a gate valve break when connected to a 2.5" discharge port on a hydrant.

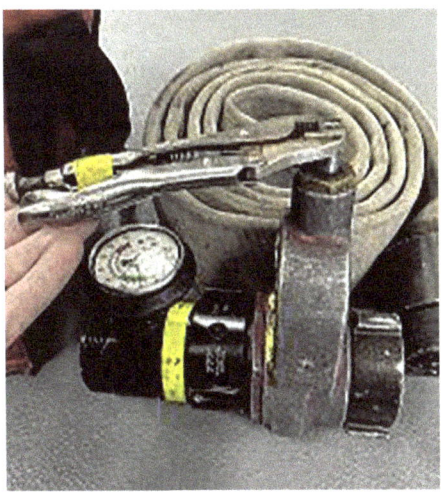

WEEK 16

Pocket of Pliers Part 3

Most fire apparatus carry an EMS kit (first-in bag) because they also provide basic life support efforts prior to the arrival of a transporting ambulance. Within their cache of gauze and airways, many stock a ring cutter for the removal of finger jewelry following trauma to a hand and/or finger.

A modern trend for men's wedding bands is for them to be made of tungsten due to its low cost and durability, which prevents them from getting scratched. The downside to the tungsten ring is that it cannot be resized, and should your hand and/or finger swell from an injury, a ring cutter will *not* work for ring removal.

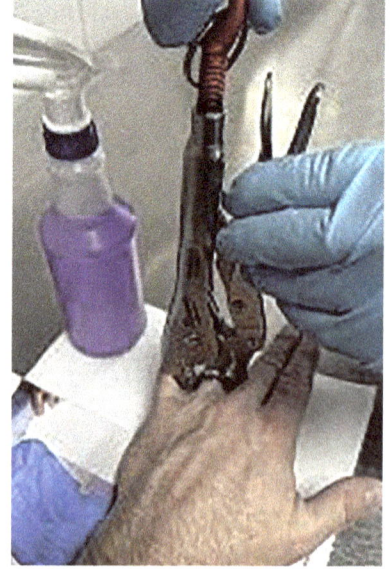

With tungsten rings, the ring itself will need to be shattered by the use of force from a pair of locking pliers. To start, capture the outside diameter of the ring with the locking pliers. Should the force *not* shatter the tungsten, open the locking pliers, adjust the eyebolt, and reapply the pliers in an effort to apply greater force. These steps should be repeated until the ring is shattered and removed. As with any practice, you need to ensure that the safety of the patient remains paramount throughout the operation to prevent further injury to the hand or finger.

WEEK 17

The Spring Clamp Part 1

This basic large spring clamp can be purchased at any local big box home improvement store for just a few dollars. While this wouldn't normally be considered a fire service tool, a lot of the equipment we use today was purposed for another task and adopted into our field.

With the spring clamp being small in nature, it can easily be stored on your person without taking up a lot of room or adding to your profile. I tend to keep one in the right exterior pocket of my bunker coat, and I clamp another to the right side bottom of my coat as well.

One of the most common uses for the spring clamp is for door control, especially for outward-swinging doors.

Once the fortified door has been compromised, place the spring clamp above the locking mechanism or doorknob and use it as a makeshift handle to control the outward-swinging door until the attack line and/or rescue team are in place and ready to enter the compartment.

With the clamp in position, the firefighter assigned to control the door can now maintain position and protection behind the door as he or she controls the door.

WEEK 18

The Spring Clamp Part 2

The door firefighter can use the spring clamp to capture the hinged side of the door to prop the door in the fixed open position while he or she backs up the hose team. An advantage of capturing the door above the middle hinge is that it is less likely to become dislodged by an advancing line, thus allowing the door to close and pinch the line.

By controlling the door in the same manner discussed above, a search team can also use the spring clamp to conduct a more effective and efficient search. With the door forced, the clamp in place, and the search team ready, the door firefighter can now control the door while the search team makes entry.

With the door in the open position, the door firefighter can now secure it in the open position by capturing the door on the hinged side (above the middle hinge) and stage at the doorway with a thermal imaging camera (TIC) to help clear the compartment faster, allowing for his or her crew to cover more ground at a rapid pace.

Whichever task you feel should take priority, using the standard spring clamp could prove to be vital in increasing the chances for a desirable outcome. The next time you are using a tool or piece of equipment from outside of the fire service, analyze its intended purpose and adapt it to the work we do on a daily basis. You never know when your take on the next trick of the trade could make the difference for another firefighter or victim.

WEEK 19

The Spring Clamp Part 3

While the Halligan tool is predominately used for truck company operations, it is being found more often now on calls for service as a tool complement (married with a Halligan bar) and implemented for forcible entry as well as for ventilation and overhaul.

Utilizing the spring clamp to marry the Halligan hook and Halligan bar helps to assist with carrying and transporting the tools from the apparatus to the door being forced. An added benefit of using the spring clamp for this purpose is that you now also have a means to control the door once the tools are separated, regardless if it is outward or inward swinging by.

WEEK 20

Ground Ladder Basics Part 1

If you are throwing a roof ladder or a multi-section ladder for ventilation or rescue, it is paramount that prior to ascending the rungs to the overhead objective, the ladder be secured at the butt (or butt spurs) by heeling or footing the ladder, which is typically taught and performed by a lone firefighter who chocks the butt with a booted foot or secures it in place by shifting their weight by placing a foot on the first rung.

While this is the most commonly taught and performed method, with staffing levels low for many responding apparatuses or the need for multiple functions to take place on the fireground, taking a firefighter "out of the fight" to heel a ladder is neither conducive to the overall objectives nor outcomes desired.

Having said that, it is crucial that firefighters learn to adapt to the staffing and surroundings they are being exposed to and find alternate means of securing the butt end of ground ladders while performing on the fireground that do *not* require the use of a staged firefighter.

Often, departments are responding to commercial properties or apartment complexes that are surrounded on multiple sides by asphalt due to the influx of needed parking to accommodate workers, patrons, or residents.

Unlike dirt or grass lawns that have the ability to sink the butt spurs into the soft soil for heeling purposes, paved lots can make it more difficult to stabilize ladders after they are thrown and prior to climbing.

Utilizing curbs and parking blocks, which are solid and fixed structures, the butt of the ladder can be left unattended, and operations can continue without staging a firefighter and taking him or her away from performing vital tasks on scene.

WEEK 21

Ground Ladder Basics Part 2

In some circumstances, paved lots might *not* have curbs or parking blocks available; however, they often have fixed objects such as railings and stanchions in place for ramps and stairs and to protect onsite services (meters, FDC, etc.).

With nothing more than a shot of 1" tubular webbing with an oversized carabiner, a thrown ladder can easily be secured in place at the correct operating angle by tying it off from a lower rung with a girth hitch and securing the working end to a railing or around a stanchion.

WEEK 22

Ground Ladder Basics Part 3

Most firefighters will dismount their respective piece of apparatus with a cache of tools and equipment, most notably a radio, flashlight, TIC, and a set of irons. Once the ladder is thrown to the target objective, the likelihood that a married set of tools will be needed for forcible entry is fairly slim, considering this will lead to performing ventilation, entering, isolating, and searching the compartment in which the ladder leads.

By utilizing the Halligan bar to heel the butt end of the ladder in conjunction with the soil, the firefighter is able to ascend the ladder with the remaining tool (a flat head axe or 6' roof hook) that can be used to take out the window and sash, sound the floor prior to entering, extend to secure the door to the compartment, and lastly, to assist with performing a successful and rapid search.

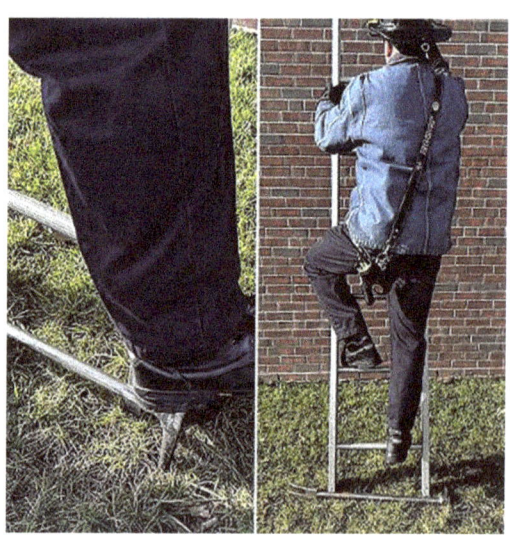

Simply place the Halligan bar at the butt of the ladder and across the width of the base with the pike toward the ground. With a booted foot, the firefighter can drive the pike into the soil, secure the ladder in place, and continue through his or her required task.

WEEK 23

The Tachometer Acronym

The fire service and EMS fields are littered with acronyms for tactics and operational needs.

Regardless of your stance on utilizing them for size up or patient care, each holds a useful purpose, and they have been found to be instrumental for many in regard to memorization and reference purposes.

A Coffee Table Quick Tip that was passed along to me when I was first promoted in a former department was found useful when responding to our mutual aid partners and better preparing myself and my crew while en route.

RPM (Radio report, Pre-incident plans, Multi-sided view)

Radio report: This will allow you to become informed of the progress of the operation or deterioration of the structure while responding, as well as what your apparatus's positioning or task will be upon arrival.

Pre-incident plans: Utilizing tablets and information provided via computer aided dispatch (CAD) systems, you can become familiar with the building construction type, size, and layout prior to arriving on scene.

Multi-sided view: Unless you are assigned to an aerial device and will be positioning at the front of the building, utilizing the *M* in the acronym will ensure that you pull past the location while observing a total of three sides of the structure to perform a portion of a 360 that can be worked in conjunction with a radio report and CAD information when developing an incident action plan (IAP) for you and your crew.

WEEK 24

Estimating the Stretch Part 1

As the first arriving engine on scene to any working fire, you can set the tone for success or failure right from the stretch, literally. Determining the length of hose to pull from the bed first is a skill set that comes with education and experience that is earned and gained in the field.

In many aspects of our job, every repetition on the fireground makes you a more effective and efficient firefighter by creating psychomotor skills that, with time, are done out of nature and habit. The cognitive learning from performing size up and understanding building construction also plays a part in making an accurate estimation when getting the first line in place.

Property boundaries for residential and commercial structures utilize fencing to secure their properties as well as to create some curbside appeal. Whether it be a vinyl privacy fence or a metal chain-link fence, the standard distance from post to post for most fencing components run every eight feet.

While pulling up to a structure from your apparatus to perform a size up, counting the number of fence posts from the engine to the door can help estimate and determine the proper length of hose that needs to be pulled from the hose bed in order to successfully make the stretch.

Having common knowledge of building construction (*ranch, cape, colonial, etc.*) combined with the number of fence posts presented is a great indicator of how much hose will be needed to reach the seat of the fire.

WEEK 25

Estimating the Stretch Part 2

As the chauffeur or company officer arrives on the engine, you can easily count the number of parking spots at a location during your approach and size up to better estimate the needed hose stretch from the apparatus to the fire floor.

The minimum size for a standard painted parking space is 9' in width and 18' long per spot, which can make for an easy estimate and round up for determining if your 200' pre-connect will make the reach.

WEEK 26

Estimating the Stretch Part 3

Acquire a 200' length of half-inch kernmantle rope and tie a butterfly knot every 50'. Place the rope into a five-gallon bucket and stage it at the pump panel of your engine, wherever the chauffeur has parked or the company officer dictates it be placed.

Stretch out the rope from a discharge port to the front door or area where access would be made to combat a fire.

Each butterfly knot is in place at the 50' mark to act as a coupling. This is a great, cost-effective, and quick training evolution that can be performed repetitively without having to strip the hose bed or take the engine out of service should a call for service arise during training.

Repacking the rope into the bucket makes for less down time during training as well as helping to get more repetitions in and capitalize on the training opportunity at hand.

WEEK 27

Size Up Variables from the Driveway Part 1

One of the most common size ups we conduct in our line of work happens when arriving on scene to a reported or confirmed structure fire. Determining the building construction and fire conditions upon arrival at a working fire all play a significant role in determining the actions that will be implemented upon arrival at the scene.

Adding into account the different variables you can determine from the motor vehicles onsite, this will allow you to conduct an enhanced size up regarding the rescue aspect of your operations. Identifying the potential quantity of victims and their age(s) are a few variables that a vehicle can provide.

It is quite common in rural America to find one vehicle per household, per adult occupying the home. Often, the number of vehicles on the property (those that appear in operable condition and are *not* on lifts or blocks) dictates the minimum number of people to expect to find while performing a primary search of the structure.

School bumper stickers or youth sports team logos on windows and rear bumpers should be taken into account to indicate that the potential for one adult and one child or teenager resides there.

WEEK 28

Size Up Variables from the Driveway Part 2

Getting a quick visual of a handicap parking permit hanging from a rearview mirror or displayed on the dashboard is a great indicator that the potential for a nonambulatory resident could still be inside the structure.

Knowing in advance that the potential exists can help determine a game plan for search and rescue right out of the gate. The resident could be wheelchair-bound, connected to electric medical equipment, and possibly using oxygen.

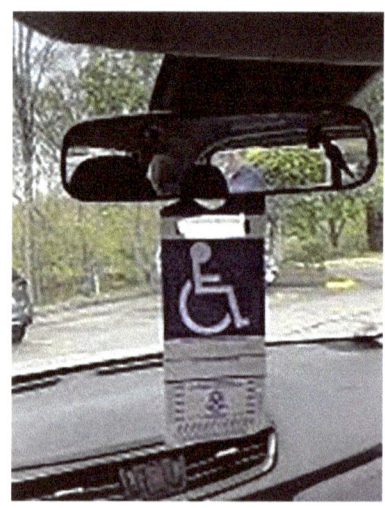

WEEK 29

Size Up Variables from the Driveway Part 3

Whether it is a four-door sedan or a gasoline-guzzling nine-passenger van, the number of seats within the motor vehicle also plays an intricate role in estimating the potential for an increased population within the structure.

Observing car seats and booster seats is a telltale sign that infants or small children reside there as well. This could play a role as to what level of maturity and competency the resident has in finding their way to an adequate egress or hiding in a closet or underneath a bed.

WEEK 30

Size Up Variables from the Driveway Part

You can normally tell a lot about a person and their habits simply by how they carry themselves regarding their physical appearance. Think of the firefighter on shift, whose bed is always made, boots are polished, and shirt is tucked in accordingly. It would be a safe assumption that they implement the same level of attention and pride in their gear and equipment as well.

 The same aspect can be said regarding the cleanliness of a vehicle's interior when relating it to hoarding conditions. When conducting your initial size up and you notice a motor vehicle cluttered with empty coffee cups, McDonald's bags, and clothes tossed throughout, it is safe to say that the interior conditions of the structure will match.

Hoarding has become a prevalent topic throughout the fire service regarding strategies, tactics, and operational hindrances. If confronted with a parked car with a similar appearance, caution must be used when conducting a primary search for the safety and well-being of the crews.

WEEK 31

Building Construction, Creating Search Aides Part 1

A senior fireman once passed on the tip of using floor vents in limited-visibility environments to find a means of egress when becoming lost or disoriented.

The placement of floor vents was originally a construction practice implemented in an effort to counter drafts and temperature changes in areas such as windows and doorways.

Identifying a floor vent can assist with navigating yourself or your crew when an immediate egress point (window or door) is needed due to deteriorating conditions.

WEEK 32

Building Construction, Creating Search Aides Part 2

The floors within a residential home provide distinct features that can assist a disoriented firefighter with identifying their location within the structure. The three most common floor coverings we find in today's homes are tile, carpet, and hardwood. Each presents its own unique feel and contour (with or without a gloved hand) that can provide a means of determining if you are in a bathroom, dining area, or bedroom.

Tiled floors can be found predominantly in bathrooms. Knowing the common layout of a raised ranch-style home and coming into contact with tile flooring, there is a high probability that you are in a room located on the upper level, on the C-side of the home.

Hooking a quick left out from the threshold of the bathroom should place you in close proximity to the stairs and toward a means of egress.

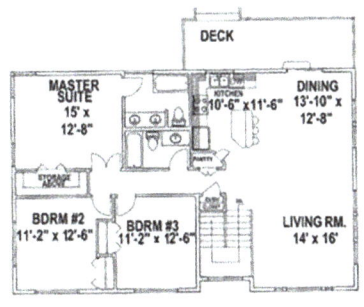

Living spaces such as bedrooms and the TV room are typically carpeted in many raised ranches around the country, with dining areas covered in hardwood flooring. Each carpeted bedroom has a minimum of one window for egress, and the dining areas often have an oversized egress point via a sliding glass door to an elevated deck area.

Familiarize yourself with the layouts and construction styles of homes in your first due while responding to routine EMS calls. This allows you to preplan the area prior to having to search these same homes with limited visibility due to smoke conditions.

WEEK 33

Practice Like You Play Part 1

One of the greatest life lessons that many of us have been taught is to "practice what you preach." It is valuable guidance that encourages all of us to lead by example and demonstrate character traits worth following.

As in everyday life, this approach also stands true in the fire service when it comes to being a mentor by taking advantage of every opportunity to train and learn. The saying "train like you play" not only applies to organized training activities; it also holds worth in taking advantage of learning opportunities found in those routine calls for service.

When responding to the run-of-the mill nuisance alarm, respond with your apparatus as you would for an assignment to a confirmed working fire. Upon arrival, utilize your apparatus as if they were chess pieces, preparing in advance for a move to conquer the opponent. The structure at hand (which is potentially on fire) is your opponent, and you want to practice and train positioning your apparatus during these routine calls in a fashion that would best suit the worst-case scenario.

For example, you respond to a commercial establishment in your first due for a fire alarm activation with no callback or confirmation. This happens on a regular basis and almost always ends with the same result: an accidental activation or system malfunction.

This is the perfect opportunity to train the way you play by strategically placing your responding apparatus in the positions most conducive to your operational needs. Pull the first arriving engine past the structure if it warrants, place the truck in front of the building, and secure a hydrant with the second due engine. Treat fire alarm activations as structure fires until proven otherwise. The more you execute these steps under normal circumstances, the more natural it will be to position apparatus correctly in an actual emergency.

WEEK 34

Practice Like You Play Part 2

Oftentimes, responding to the same address repeatedly and being met with the same results will create a sense of complacency among responders. Far too often, I have witnessed seasoned firefighters respond to alarm activations donning only their bunker pants or arriving with their jacket wide open and not a single ounce of urgency in their steps. Worse than this, their actions are showing the less experienced firefighters that it is an acceptable practice.

Would you show up for a job interview wearing your gym attire or your Sunday best? Dressing for success means being prepared for battle 100 percent of the time.

Make it a challenge: turning each response into a forty-five–second drill not only creates an atmosphere of friendly competition among the crew but also instills the importance and efficiency of donning the required personal protective equipment (PPE). When the time comes that the routine alarm is an actual fire, you will be dressed for success.

For many company officers who I have had the pleasure of working for, any and all calls for service warranted the need for a diligent response while donning *all* of the required PPE up until the point it was deemed safe to remove it. Actions like that made us ready for whatever circumstances we would be met with upon arrival and through further investigation.

WEEK 35

Practice Like You Play Part 3

At the start of every shift, it is critical to make sure all crew members understand what their job function or riding assignment will be for the duration of the shift. Knowing what role you will play and how to properly perform these tasks is a great way to eliminate duplication of efforts and avoid assumptions that someone else is taking care of a particular task.

While responding to the scene for a fire alarm activation, plan out in advance what tools and equipment will be needed to fulfill the position you have been assigned, so that when the same response turns into a structure fire, everyone is already in the game.

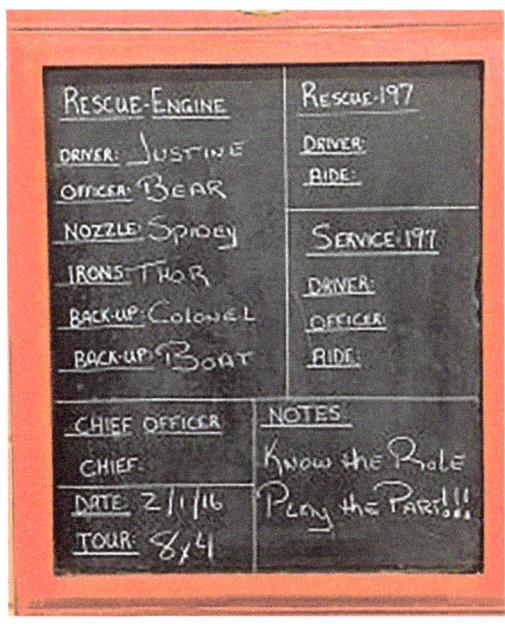

WEEK 36

Practice Like You Play Part 4

By far, the greatest advantage of routine responses is the opportunity to perform informal preplanning of the target hazards in your first due district. Although you are operating on an actual scene, you are in a less critical mode of response, which allows personnel to focus on important information that will be valuable during a more serious response.

If you are a backstep firefighter, you will not have many opportunities to perform fire inspections and preplanning. What better way to familiarize yourself with the structures than to train by playing the CONE game at every location you respond to, both residential and commercial?

The acronym CONE stands for Construction-type, Occupancy, Number of floors, and Entrance/Exits. By knowing the type of *construction* of a building, you will be better prepared for how fire behavior could affect the structure.

Knowing the *occupancy* of the structure will play a huge role in determining life safety and suppression concerns and challenges.

Knowing the *number of floors* in the structure is critical for your own safety. This bit of information will determine the length of the hose stretch you will pull, the distance you will travel into the structure with what air supply you have in your SCBA, and what information is needed for area familiarization should you become lost or disoriented inside of the structure.

Lastly, identifying the location and number of *entrance points and exits* is important for the accountability of occupants as well as for firefighters who may need to exit the building rapidly via an alternate means than the primary exit.

Week 37

Bleach Bottle of Rope

For many of the apartment structures within our response area, the option exists where an upper-level hose advancement can be done utilizing a back porch stretch. An officer or firefighter equipped with a thermal imaging camera (TIC), a set of forcible entry tools, and a rope bottle can easily investigate and place a line into operation should the conditions warrant it.

The *rope bottle* consists of an old bleach bottle, 40' of 11 mil life safety rope, and a large carabiner. Take the tool cache of the TIC, forcible entry tools, and rope bottle with you for investigations on a second floor or greater. If you identify a need for a hose line to extinguish an area with extension or need to address exposure concerns, the carabiner and rope can be thrown down to the pump operator who can then hook the carabiner to the bale of the nozzle for hoisting rather than you retreating back down to the street.

A few key benefits:

- A shorter length of hose can be stretched.
- There is less opportunity for kinks or couplings to get caught on the stairs.
- Leaves the stairwell and porch steps open for egress or additional crews.

WEEK 38

Stair Stretches

In previous *Coffee Table Quick Tips*, we discussed various methods of estimating your hose stretch by utilizing elements of the scene, such as marked parking spaces and installed fence lines.

Another quick reference that was passed down to me was the DOSE acronym:

> D: Distance from the engine to the structure
> O: Obstacles such as topography and fixed objects
> S: Stairs (corkscrew, return stairs, wellhole, etc.)
> E: Elevation refers to the number of floors between the entrance and the fire.

A good guideline for needed lengths when a stretch involves *stairs*:

- 50' hose length: two floors for corkscrew stairs
- 50' hose length: one set of return stairs
- 50' hose length: five floors for wellholes

WEEK 39

Water Supply, at Nine O'clock

Working and responding in an area equipped with fire hydrants is a fortunate instance due to the ease of the water supply engine being able to secure a municipal water supply for suppression efforts once arriving on scene.

While coming up through the ranks, I was shown a number of tricks of the trade from senior firefighters regarding the steps of being a "Plug Firefighter" and how I could use those tricks to become efficient at the role.

Many of the actions taught revolved around wrapping the hydrant, flushing for debris, and even positioning the gates for simplicity to prevent the hydrant wrench from contacting the gate wheel while operating the hydrant knuckle.

A Coffee Table Quick Tip regarding hydrants that has stood out over the past twenty-five years is the nine o'clock trick when  removing the steamer cap that seems to have been tightened too much, seized with rust or paint, or potentially frozen from moisture and exterior temperatures.

Placing the hydrant wrench in the nine o'clock position allows you to work smarter and not harder by capitalizing on using your body weight in conjunction with the wrench positioning.

The same concept can be utilized when shutting the hydrant down and securing the steamer cap prior to leaving the scene. Place the wrench in the three o'clock position and use your body weight to secure the cap in place.

The longer it takes to remove the caps and dress them with the associated appliances, the longer it takes to establish and secure a water supply. This Coffee Table Quick Tip helps to ensure the task gets completed in a timely manner while also placing ergonomics as a priority and preventing injuries.

WEEK 40

Tool Trick Part 1

At the room of origin and ran out of door chocks?!? Then go ahead and use the set of irons you brought to the door, place the flat head axe as shown in the photo below to prop the door in the open position, and secure it in place with a tap or two from your Halligan.

By placing the axe in this manner, with the handle following the direction of the handline, the axe now serves a few purposes:

- The flat head of the axe holds the door open for handline advancement.

- The handle can be used as an aid or guide when determining if the open door is a wall or door in limited-visibility environments.
- If an officer stages at the door with a TIC while a primary is conducted, he or she can place the handle off the door at a forty-five degree angle to extend themselves into the room a few more feet without compromising their situational awareness and area familiarization.
- Should conditions outside the room or compartment deteriorate and warrant the door to close, the handle can easily be grabbed, pulling the head free from the base of the floor.

Week 41

Tool Trick Part 2

The Halligan bar is as useful and reliable as it has been since 1948, and it can be used during suppression, search, ventilation, technical rescue, equipment/machine stabilization, and self-rescue. The Halligan bar's design can be implemented during a search to help identify and change the grade or void space.

By extending the Halligan bar ahead of you (adz end out) while advancing in a low or crawling position, the weight of the adz end will cause the bar to shift when the adz end slides over a hole in the floor, comes into contact with a stair riser, or, more importantly, when you approach an unforeseen stair tread leading down a flight of stairs.

In limited-visibility situations, the Halligan bar can act as an added sense to make you aware of what you are unable to see.

The Halligan bar has stood the test of time—the test of sweat, smoke, and soot. There is a reason why this tool has been around for close to seventy years. Learn how to use it, become proficient with it, and you will reap its many benefits on the incident scene.

WEEK 42

Tool Trick Part 3

In vehicle fires and motor vehicle collisions, oftentimes the mechanical means of supporting the hood in the open position will be compromised. The Halligan bar can easily be used to prop open and secure the hood while battery terminals are secured or extinguishment is completed.

The old saying, "If it ain't broke, don't fix it," holds true. The Halligan bar is as useful and reliable as it has been since 1948, and it can be used during suppression, search, ventilation, technical rescue, equipment/machine stabilization, and self-rescue.

WEEK 43

Tool Trick Part 4

The Halligan hook can easily be implemented for use in forcing an inward swinging door in the same manner as that of the adz end of a Halligan bar.

Displayed in the photo below is a great tip that was passed on to me that focuses on the tool doing most of the work due to the increase in leverage with the size of the hook.

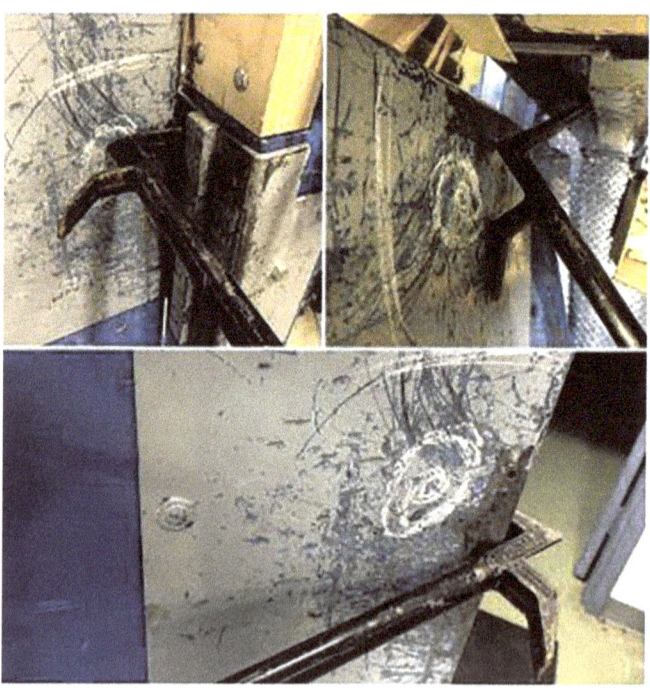

The end of the Halligan hook provides leverage between the panel and the jamb and creates approximately 4 1/2" of spread compared to 6" of spread when using the adz end of the Halligan bar.

Once the door is forced, utilize the same Halligan hook to pull the door back toward the frame until you have a line in place and are ready to advance into the structure or specific compartment or room.

WEEK 44

Gemtor Harness and SCBA Conversion

In many organizations, a lot of firefighters are equipped with a traditional Gemtor harness or some form of integrated system. By utilizing the components of the SCBA harness and the attached Gemtor, a three-point hauling device can be created rather quickly with the limited dexterity of a gloved hand and prove to be quite effective in preventing a downed firefighter from being stripped from their air pack while being hauled from an IDLH environment.

1. Start by unbuckling the waist strap of the SCBA harness.
2. Feed each end up through the front leg straps of the harness.
3. Reconnect the buckle mechanism (for integrated systems, this step can be skipped or the waist strap can be fed between the legs and captured or buckled at the groin area).
4. Join the SCBA shoulder straps with the oversized Gemtor carabiner.

This basic pack conversion can prove to be beneficial when hauling or lowering a downed firefighter via a mechanical advantage and can act as a three-point harness, securing them in the event they become inverted during their removal from a structure.

WEEK 45

Pre-Rigged Hauling System for a Downed Firefighter

With this week's Coffee Table Quick Tip, we are going to introduce the idea and concept of utilizing a pre-rigged mechanical advantage along with a thrown extension ladder or aerial device as an overhead anchor point.

By combining minimal hardware and a half-inch kernmantle life safety rope, a system can be implemented into the rescue of a downed firefighter by hauling him or her down a hallway to a window and lowering him or her to the ground in a controlled manner.

Equipment Needed:

- 100' of ½" kernmantle life safety rope
- three oversized carabiners
- two single pulleys
- extension ladder

Throw the appropriate-sized extension ladder to the window designated for rescue or egress, and make sure it extends up and over the top of the window with the system attached to a rung that is higher than the top of the window.

Using the center pulley and oversized carabiner, attach it to the SCBA harness of the downed firefighter and use this system to lift the downed firefighter (after his or her pack has been converted to a three-point harness) up and over the windowsill, then, in a controlled manner, lower to the ground where he or she can be attended to further.

In some circumstances, the downed firefighter may find it rather difficult to drag or push down a hallway to the window due to their physical size, the added weight of their gear, or minimal staffing on scene. With the ladder and system in place, the downed firefighter can be hauled to the window with the system as long as the crew performing the rescue has the ability to grab the center pulley and oversized carabiner from the window opening after the ladder has been put into place.

WEEK 46

Identifying Bedroom Windows During Size Up

Residential structures are built and framed out with windows for a wide array of reasons, with the main dedication being to introduce natural lighting, to provide a viewing point, to be used for natural ventilation, and also as a means of egress in the event of an emergency.

With the exception of storage areas such as closets and/or attached garages, *all* occupied rooms in residential construction will be equipped with a window.

Statistics have shown that a total of 45 percent of rescues are made via bedroom windows. With that statistic in mind, it is imperative that we are able to quickly identify and ladder windows in residential structures that are habitable or bedrooms during fire suppression activities.

Bedroom windows are easy to identify due to building code requirements and common residential floor plans. These windows typically have a diagonal measurement of approximately four feet, which allows for firefighters to enter and residents to egress.

Having intimate knowledge and familiarization with building code requirements and the construction styles that make up your first due response area is a critical skill that every officer and firefighter should continue to hone in on.

When responding to a fire at a residential structure, on-scene crews need to make every effort to ladder every window above the ground floor and every window that appears to be that of a bedroom.

WEEK 47

Commercial Roof Structure— Creating Saw Access

When existing fixtures such as vent fans and skylights to vertically ventilate the roof of a commercial structure aren't available, it is up to the crew working on the roof to determine the construction makeup of the roofing material as well as what the most effective and efficient means of "opening up" the roof might be.

With many modern commercial structures, such as supermarkets and big box stores, being built throughout the country, the roof is comprised of various layers of decking and material, such as metal corrugated sheathing, often topped with insulation and vapor barriers, as well as a waterproofing layer.

 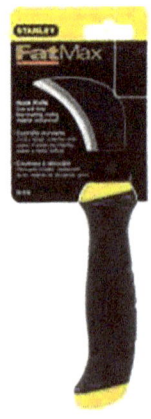

Prior to implementing your rotary saw and attempting to cut the decking, it would be advantageous on our part to remove the top membrane (rubber and adhesive waterproofing layer) to better determine if the decking is in fact made of metal corrugated sheets or if it is a poured slab.

A cost-effective tool that can easily be carried on your person or attached to the handle of a rotary saw is a fixed-blade linoleum knife, as seen in the photo above. Stanley makes a 3" Fat-Max Fixed Knife that can easily be used to cut the top membrane free to inspect the layers or decking below to better determine what type of saw and/or blade will be needed.

WEEK 48

Identifying a Parapet from Below

Preplanning structures in your first due is the most proactive and advantageous move a fire officer can do to better prepare themselves and their crews for a response to properties such as warehouses, grocery stores, and storage facilities.

When performing walkthroughs, time is often invested with attention focused on the type(s) of building construction along with the best apparatus access, riser room location, roof access, hazardous storage, and ventilation systems involved.

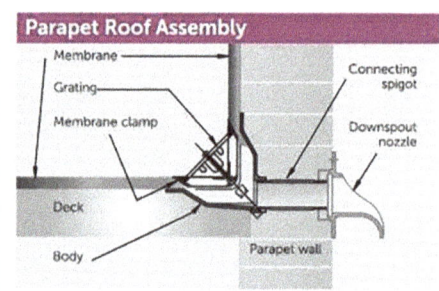

When planning for the truck company, make sure to locate and identify the drainage system for the roof in an effort to determine whether or not a parapet exists on the roof and, if so, what the drop-off distance is for those ascending to the roof.

While on scene and setting up to ladder the building from the turntable of your aerial device, look for downspout nozzles or scuppers, which will provide a clear identifying marker to where the flat roof exists on the hidden side of the parapet wall and prevent a fall while climbing up and over.

WEEK 49

Existing Drainage, Water Removal from the Structure

During fire suppression activities, copious amounts of water are pumped into a structure, which, over time, accumulates and creates further hazards than the initial fire at hand.

With water weighing approximately 8.35 lbs. a gallon, the potential for a floor collapse increases dramatically with the added weight or load placed on the floor, which has already been compromised by heat and charring.

Rather than hauling cumbersome hoses and pumps to the area impacted so the water can be evacuated rapidly, you can easily utilize the installed plumbing and piping to remove the water by simply removing the toilet from the flange.

With most toilets being made from porcelain, this task can be accomplished by smashing the toilet with a flat head axe, Halligan bar, or sledge hammer.

Remember to secure the domestic water supply to the toilet to prevent further accumulation of water in the immediate area.

WEEK 50

The Thermal Imaging Camera for Open Water Spills

The TIC has proven its usefulness time and time again for first responders when operating at structure fires. Introducing TIC use at hazardous materials incidents provides a tactical advantage that can help reduce some of the guessing games firefighters are faced with when confronting the unknowns we often encounter at these incidents.

Example

A motorboat leaked an unknown amount of oil into the water after having motor malfunctions. The operator calls the local fire department to respond. The sun is going down, and visibility is now becoming limited.

How can you better determine the extent and impact of the spill? Looking at the surface of the body of water through the TIC, you will see the footprint left behind by the oil spill by observing different heat signatures on the TIC display.

This "footprint" will help show the size of the area that needs to be contained and/or cleaned.

WEEK 51

Brown Smoke, Bad Building

Being versed in the four separate qualities of smoke will better prepare you as a company officer or firefighter when developing and implementing an incident action plan (IAP) on the fireground.

The four attributes are as follows: (1) volume, (2) velocity, (3) density and (4) color.

For this week's Coffee Table Quick Tip, I want to touch on the color of smoke present at a fire, and more importantly, *brown*-colored smoke.

Smoke that is brown in color is a strong indicator that the structural members (unfinished wood) of a wood-built building or ordinary construction are burning.

When this is present, it is a sign that the fire has grown from the contents of the building and is now burning the structure itself, which in turn compromises the structural integrity of the roof, wall, and floor components.

With the presence of brown smoke, the decision to change the IAP needs to be entertained, and for the overall safety of personnel operating inside the structure, an immediate evacuation should be performed.

In the photo above, brown smoke could be seen

emitting from the soffit, which was the signal present that warranted an evacuation of the building, which was met shortly after with the collapse of the roof's structural members and associated sheathing.

WEEK 52

The "Odor Unfounded" Call for Service

Time and time again, we find ourselves responding to the "smell of an electrical fire" in residential environments that are met with an odor and a slight smoke condition (haze) but are unable to locate the source.

    Before writing it off and reporting "unfounded" over your portable radio, take a minute and check the dishwasher for a spatula or plastic lid that has found its way down to the heating element of the dishwasher.

    The melted plastic creates the same odor and smoke conditions that we are often met with while responding to electrical fires.

Conclusion

It is my hope that the result of this small project can assist the reader with developing an addition to their current training curriculum and, in turn, continuing to pass along just a few tips of the trade, fifty-two to be exact, that have been taught to me during my tenure in the greatest profession known to man.

With each Coffee Table Quick Tip that is read, implemented, and passed down to the next firefighter, the legacy of those who have paved the way for our individual journeys will live on for generations to come.

While some of the tips might be conducive to a specific geographical location, a predetermined standard operating policy (SOP), or even derived from a particular staffing allotment, each Coffee Table Quick Tip can easily be adapted to fit the needs of your specific department.

The Coffee Table Quick Tip you read this week might not be relevant to a call for service you encounter during the next twenty-four-hour tour, but when the day arises and you pull a tip out from the back of your brain while at a run, it could very well make the difference in a successful outcome for all parties involved.

Somewhere along the line of your time in the fire service, others took the time to invest in you. Do the right thing and pay their legacy forward by passing that same knowledge onto others.

About the Author

AB Turenne is a twenty-five-year veteran of the fire service and is currently the captain of training and safety with a career department in Middlesex County, Connecticut.

As a Certified Level III Fire Service Instructor, AB's training curriculum has proven to be conducive to the operational needs of those he has taught, which in turn has improved the human capital knowledge of many.

A graduate of the master of public administration program at Anna Maria College, AB has continued his efforts in training and education by contributing to fire engineering and other reputable resources.

AB resides in Middlesex County, Connecticut, with his wife Renee, who is an elementary school teacher, and their three children: Gianna, Dominic, and Noella.

Printed in the USA
CPSIA information can be obtained
at www.ICGtesting.com
CBHW051104250924
14860CB00046BA/489